CAPRICORN

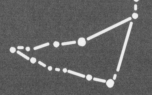

A GUIDED JOURNAL

Constance Stellas

ADAMS MEDIA
New York London Toronto Sydney New Delhi

Adams Media
An Imprint of Simon & Schuster, Inc.
100 Technology Center Drive
Stoughton, Massachusetts 02072

First Adams Media hardcover edition September 2022

ADAMS MEDIA and colophon are trademarks of Simon & Schuster.

For information about special discounts for bulk purchases, please contact Simon & Schuster Special Sales at 1-866-506-1949 or business@simonandschuster.com.

The Simon & Schuster Speakers Bureau can bring authors to your live event. For more information or to book an event contact the Simon & Schuster Speakers Bureau at 1-866-248-3049 or visit our website at www.simonspeakers.com.

Interior design by Colleen Cunningham
Interior illustrations by Tess Armstrong
Interior images © Getty Images/Vikiss, Mara Fribus; Simon & Schuster, Inc.

Manufactured in China

10 9 8 7 6 5 4 3 2 1

ISBN 978-1-5072-1950-8

CONTENTS

INTRODUCTION

Are you interested in how the stars may influence your characteristics? Wanting a little celestial insight into how you can strengthen your relationships? Looking for guidance in using your determination and spirituality? Guided journaling can be a dialogue between your thoughts, feelings, and aspects of your sign and element. By reflecting in an intentional way, you can begin to understand yourself—and how you interact with the world around you—better.

An earth sign, Capricorn begins on the winter solstice, also called the World Point. The solstice marks both the longest night and the sun's slow climb toward increasing daylight. It is a powerful energetic time that emphasizes Capricorn's light and dark traits as well as her leadership abilities. Journaling can help you understand your darker fears and move toward the eternal hope and light that your sign possesses. Have you ever felt so driven to get something that you blocked out other aspects of your life, such as health? Or fun? The prompts in this book allow you to cultivate more balance—while still achieving your goals— by exploring your Capricorn tendencies and what you may share with other earth signs.

Journaling can also help you keep in touch with your feelings so you can sense which opportunities and people will be fortuitous and helpful. Capricorn is symbolized by the sea goat, which combines the durable strength of a goat on land and the emotional sensitivity of a fish in the sea. The shadow side of her abilities is brushing off spontaneity and sticking to the rules no matter what. This rigidity can mask her softer and more spiritual qualities. Are you known for doggedly going after the things you want? In tune with your feelings—and the feelings of others? By reflecting on the prompts in this book, you will gain a deeper understanding of what has and hasn't helped you deal with others and learn how to integrate both structure *and* emotional wisdom into all phases of your life.

When you write, you connect with your feelings, desires, and everything in between. And when prompts drive you to contemplate the wealth of astrological wisdom that each element and Sun sign offers, it can lead to surprising, creative insights. Maybe you recognized your abilities to structure practical life but didn't know that this structure can also help others to get organized and achieve their goals too. Or perhaps you never considered how your dry wit can lighten even the most serious situations. This book will help you explore yourself and your place among the stars.

HOW TO USE THIS BOOK

Welcome to your astrology journal! This guided journal is divided into three parts to help you explore your connections to the stars.

PART ONE

First, there are prompts about astrology in general, from how you feel about astrological wisdom to what you notice about your relationships with different signs and your experiences with reading horoscopes. The long and rich history of astrology can truly enhance your life and deepen your self-knowledge. Whatever strikes your fancy is a prompt to pursue! The purpose is not to master celestial knowledge but to turn your thoughts to the cosmos and reflect in an intentional way that may uncover some surprising insights.

PART TWO

The second part features prompts about your element. In astrology, there are four elements:

- Fire
- Earth
- Air
- Water

There are three zodiac signs in each element.

THE PASSIONATE FIRE SIGNS ARE:	ARIES	LEO	SAGITTARIUS

THE PRACTICAL EARTH SIGNS ARE:	TAURUS	VIRGO	CAPRICORN

THE COMMUNICATIVE AIR SIGNS ARE:	GEMINI	LIBRA	AQUARIUS

THE EMOTIONAL WATER SIGNS ARE:	CANCER	SCORPIO	PISCES

All members of the same element have an affinity; being with your elemental brothers or sisters can often feel comfortable because they speak your language. Understanding the characteristics of your element can give insight into good health practices and ways to relax and recharge, as well as how you might approach aspects of life such as work and relationships.

PART THREE

Finally, the third part of this journal concentrates on your Sun sign. This is the position of the sun when you were born. The Sun sign is a dominant feature in a person's entire chart. It reveals your:

- Psychological characteristics
- Health habits
- Relationship affinities
- Spiritual mission in this lifetime

Each Sun sign also has a ruling planet that gives the sign a certain kind of energy; a symbol that represents the characteristics of the sign's personality; and a modality that reveals whether that sign charges ahead in life, prefers the security of things remaining the same, or is open to the changes that come along. Consider these prompts intuitively. When something speaks to you and you think "Yes! That's me," reflect on the questions and any suggestions posed by the prompt. If you don't feel particularly drawn to a prompt, you may want to return to it later. If the information or questions in a prompt make you feel uncomfortable, consider whether there is something hidden or suppressed in your life that it awakens. Or you may use the page to explore why this doesn't fit you. True, not every aspect of the Sun sign will resonate with every person, so you may want to look at your full birth chart to help color the portrait of you that you create in this journal.

Astrology has become more and more popular, thanks to the ease of calculating birth charts online; the availability of daily, weekly, or monthly horoscopes delivered straight to your inbox; popular lists of famous people according to their Sun signs; and more. Ancient astrologers may have appreciated these options, *but* a computer is not a person, and the information that computer printouts offer is standard. Anyone born on the same day, time, year, and place as you would have the same astrology chart; however, people are individuals. There's a lot more to you than what is written about a Sun sign or astrological element. The beauty of this journal is that you can reflect on what astrology means to *you* and understand the nuances of your sign and element and how they do or don't relate to you as a unique person. Use this journal as your guide in exploring what the stars can teach you about yourself!

Astrology is the study of star and planetary patterns and what they mean for individuals and societies. Observing the regular motions of the sun, the moon, and other planets, ancient people became adept at interpreting what these celestial bodies and cycles meant. Today, there is a new renaissance in astrology, thanks to the Internet. Now anyone can find out the locations of the sun, the moon, Venus, and more at the time of their birth in just seconds, and subscribe to a service featuring daily, weekly, and monthly astrological forecasts. Consulting astrologers also offer star wisdom for health, business dealings, romance, spiritual development, and marriage.

In this part, you'll find thought-provoking prompts to guide you in reflecting on astrology in a more general context, rather than focusing on one specific sign or element. The sun, the moon, Mercury, Venus, Mars, Jupiter, Saturn, Uranus, Neptune, and Pluto: All of these celestial energies make up a natal chart and become a blueprint for gaining deeper self-knowledge and guiding your life. You can explore the astrological patterns in your family, track how different events like eclipses and equinoxes impact your mood and experiences, consider your beliefs on fate versus free will, and more. Enjoy this journey into the cosmos.

PART ONE

GETTING TO KNOW THE WORLD OF ASTROLOGY

Imagine you are lying on the grass or a beach or sitting on a bench at night. You can see the stars, perhaps the moon. Depending on the time of year, you might even see Venus twinkling on the horizon or a distant red glow from Mars. Describe what you feel. Awe? Like you are part of the universe? Or like you are insignificant compared to the vast celestial sky? Maybe curious to know more about the heavens?

If you were an ancient navigator and only had the constellations and the moon with which to navigate your ship to get home, would you feel comforted by the regularity of the patterns in the night sky? Write about a time when you felt lost literally or emotionally. Did the moon or a twinkling star give you courage? Did you notice if the moon during that time was just a crescent or full? Or maybe it was somewhere in between?

Astrology has become more and more popular in recent years, thanks to the Internet! Do you believe that everything astrology says about your sign is true? Write about a positive experience you have had reading your horoscope. Did you follow the advice? What happened?

What charms you about astrology? What bothers or concerns you about it? Are you mindful of the monthly zodiac sign changes? Describe any feelings you have about how certain zodiac time periods affect you. For example, in spring, when the sun is in Aries, maybe you feel energized.

Are there certain signs with which you are more harmonious? Less harmonious? Write about your experiences.

A person's fate or destiny is a lifelong path. Describe how you feel when you read an astrological prediction for your future. Do you think it is good to know this information? Or better not to know? Do you use this information, keep it in mind, or ignore it?

Each zodiac sign is ruled by a planet or by the Sun or the Moon. Do you identify with Mercury, Venus, Mars, Jupiter, Saturn, Uranus, Neptune, Pluto, the Sun, or the Moon? Is it the planet your sign is ruled by? If not, describe your feelings about your own sign's planet. Do you think knowing more about your planet brings you insights into your personality or fortune?

The most famous—or infamous!—astrological event is Mercury Retrograde. This happens three times each year and means that Mercury appears to be moving backward in relation to the earth's orbit. It is common during these periods to experience electronic mishaps, communications going awry, and difficulties and delays in scheduling. Describe any Mercury Retrograde experiences you may have noticed. Were you forced to be more patient than usual?

If your Sun is in Gemini or Virgo, both signs ruled by Mercury, you may experience more personal confusion during Mercury in retrograde. Describe any personal confusion that you or your Gemini or Virgo friends experience at this time. Did you notice that you or they felt relief when Mercury was no longer retrograde?

The moon is our closest celestial neighbor, and its rhythms influence daily life. The monthly new moon marks the beginning of the moon's phases. At the new moon, people make wishes or set intentions with support from the moon's increasing energy as she waxes toward the full moon (the peak of lunar energy). Do you tend to notice the moon's phase, influence, or sign? Write about your relationship with and feeling toward this light.

Many astrologers believe that a person's chart can indicate past lives. What historical time period do you feel connected to? Who do you feel you might have been in a past life? What was your profession? Do you believe a past life can influence your present life? If so, how?

Each astrological sign is either masculine or feminine. This designation has nothing to do with gender or sexual orientation. The masculine signs radiate outwardly, and the feminine signs inwardly. Make a list of all the signs in your birth chart. Which energy dominates? Or perhaps they are equal? Do you feel these descriptions are true to your self-image?

In astrology, each sign has a symbol associated with it. Think about the symbol for your sign. Explore your feelings toward this symbol. Do any of its characteristics apply to you? You might write a story about yourself and what your symbol means to you. For example, as a Leo, are you more like a roaring lion or a purring cat?

As you will discover in this guided journey, there are four elements: fire, earth, air, and water. Each sign belongs to one element. Have you noticed that the signs of people you get along with have the same element as you do? Or a certain different element? Write about your experiences with people of the same and different elements.

Some people believe that following astrology curtails free will by forecasting the future. Do you believe this? Do you think it is possible that by knowing about your sign and using the stars as guides for the future you can make better choices in your life? Or do you feel controlled by what the stars say? Reflect on your feelings about free will and the stars.

Throughout the history of astrology, healers and physicians were required to study the positions of the planets in order to help their patients. They believed that the planetary energies could help or hinder healing the soul and body. What do you think about this idea? Can you implement any of your astrological insights into your health practices?

The position of the sun, the moon, and the ascendant are the three most important placements in a person's natal chart. If you know your birth time, you can easily determine these with the help of an app or astrology website. Explore your astrological trio and write down your feelings about these placements. Do you feel more connected to your moon or to your ascendant? Are there any patterns you notice, like the same element for each placement?

Eclipses were awesome phenomena for the ancients—and still have us in awe today! In a total solar eclipse, the sun's light is blocked by the moon, and the atmosphere darkens. In a lunar eclipse, the moon is blocked by the earth, and we cannot see this silvery orb. Most years have four eclipses. Do you pay attention to this heavenly event? Do you notice any patterns, either within yourself or in your surroundings during an eclipse? Research when the next eclipse will be, and record your feelings for the week leading up to the event.

How do you typically "use" astrology? Do you find it useful for self-understanding? Understanding other people? Exploring your friendships and/or partnerships? Do daily horoscopes guide your actions? Or do you see astrology as more of a guide for larger focuses in life? Write about an experience when an astrological tip helped you in some way.

Have you noticed that people in the same family often have the same signs? Or that other positions in their charts correspond? It's frequently the case! Take a look at your family's and extended family's signs, and reflect on the similarities and differences.

Saturn is the farthest planet you can see with the naked eye. It rules time, structure, and lessons of life. A major astrological transit is the Saturn Return, when Saturn returns to its natal chart position. This happens between ages twenty-eight and thirty. Where is Saturn in your chart? Have you experienced this return? Whether you have experienced your Saturn Return or not, write about your feelings toward the current path of your life, relationships, health, and spiritual development. If you have experienced your Saturn Return, how did your life look during these years?

Aside from your Saturn Return, another important transit (when a planet returns to its original position in your birth chart) is with the planet Jupiter. Jupiter is called the benefic of the zodiac. He helps us feel generous toward ourselves and others, is good for business, and can bring new areas of creativity into life. Jupiter returns to his birthplace every twelve years. Think about your birthday years at each twelfth year so far. Write about your feelings and activities in those years. Were the experiences positive? Expansive? Creative?

The solstices, summer and winter, occur at opposite signs: Cancer in the summer, and Capricorn in the winter. They mark the height of sunlight in summer and the depths of darkness in winter. How is your mood at these times? Describe how these essential astrological markers affect you.

Two major points in nature and the celestial calendar are the equinoxes: the fall equinox (Libra) and the spring equinox (Aries). These events mean there is equal daylight and darkness during that day. Do you have any particular feelings during these times of the year? Happy fall is coming after a hot summer? Or anticipating spring after a harsh winter? Write your feelings about the rhythm of nature and how it corresponds to your experience of the seasons. If you live in the southern hemisphere, the equinoxes are reversed.

If someone you know says, "I don't believe in astrology, it's rubbish," what do you say back? Write a dialogue between you and a skeptical person. What are your points of agreement? Of disagreement?

Have you ever noticed that some days feel lucky and positive and that during other days nothing seems to go right? It could be that the planetary pattern in the sky is not in harmony with your personal planets! Keep a record of good and bad days and the placements of the planets during each day. Reflect on any patterns. (You can find the daily position of the planets online.)

Throughout history, people have sought to understand the world around them. Today we have scientific equipment to inform us of the makeup of the universe, but ancient peoples could only observe the basic elements that they saw in their lives: fire, earth, air, and water. They associated each of these elements with an astrological sign and certain characteristics, and physicians used these characteristics to treat and heal their patients. The elements and their characteristics are:

FIRE (Aries, Leo, Sagittarius): Fire signs are known for their passionate energy and impetuosity. They often need to moderate their bursts of enthusiasm to prevent burnout.

EARTH (Taurus, Virgo, Capricorn): Earth signs are practical, cautious, and seek out security with a measured pace. Cultivating change and taking a few risks can enhance their lives, boost their health, and encourage flexibility.

AIR (Gemini, Libra, Aquarius): Air signs are changeable and mentally oriented; they enjoy living in creative possibilities and have highly sensitive nervous systems. Getting "down to earth" can help air signs move forward realistically.

WATER (Cancer, Scorpio, Pisces): Water is the element of feelings, and all water signs react to life emotionally. Calming their waves of emotion in order to see a situation clearly is a lifelong challenge for all water signs.

The more than two dozen prompts in this part of the book will give you a platform for understanding more about yourself and your nature based on your element.

PART TWO

GETTING TO KNOW YOUR ELEMENT

Earth is our most familiar element. It is where we live and where we are connected to the practical aspects of life. "Be grounded," "feet on the ground," "down-to-earth": These are all expressions of the earth's hold on us. Write about your feelings regarding Planet Earth. Do you feel connected here? Happy in the place where you live?

There are many myths in different cultures about the creation of the earth. Most feature a Mother Earth figure, like Mother Nature. In Greek mythology, Gaia is the Earth Mother who emerged from cosmic chaos and gave birth to Ouranos, the sky god. "Protecting Gaia" is an expression used by modern ecology and environmental students to describe the interrelatedness of all plants, animals, minerals, and humans on Earth. Write your impressions about how people are currently interacting with Gaia. Are you involved in any groups related to helping the planet? Do you have a personal feeling about our home, Gaia?

Earth signs are levelheaded, concrete thinkers, and pragmatic. They favor practical solutions to problems. They like to measure success and progress. Does this describe you? How do you measure success and progress?

Earth is the element most associated with agriculture. A garden, vegetable patch, or fields of grain are all bounty from the earth! Do you garden? Grow plants? Describe any experiences you have had with agriculture or house plants. Do you have a favorite way to connect to agriculture or horticulture?

Earth signs—unlike the idea-oriented air signs, the passionate fire signs, or the fluid water signs—want to know "how do we accomplish our project?" Imagine you are the earth team leader with an air, fire, and water sign on your team. How do you gather the team to work together? How do you own your leadership role? Describe your plan for getting things done.

The seasons of spring, summer, autumn, and winter are the natural calendar and rhythm of the earth. Which season do you feel most connected to? Describe your feelings about this season, as well as the remaining seasons. Are there any special activities that you do in your spare time during each season?

Different areas of the earth bring out different feelings in people. Which areas do you prefer—urban or rural? Mountains or deserts? What climate suits you the best? What kinds of climates have you lived in, at different times of your life? Which place was/is the most comfortable?

In astrology, there is a technique called astrocartography. In this technique, the astrologer overlays a person's natal chart on a world map to see where harmonious and inharmonious locations are. Interesting! Where do you imagine your harmonious zone is? Are there any places that have been difficult to live in or visit? Concentrate on your feeling about the geography rather than the people.

Building—whether bridges, homes, churches, or monuments—is an earth activity. This is the way humans protect themselves from weather or celebrate the beauty of architecture and progress. Imagine the most beautiful, practical, and useful building you can. What would it look like? Where would it be? Write down your vision and how you might go about building this structure.

Caves with crystals, stalactites, and stalagmites run deep into the earth. Some caves even have rivers flowing through them! Have you ever visited a cave? Did you notice the peace and quiet? The cool, dark atmosphere? Write about any experiences you have had in caves. If you've never been to a cave, how do you feel about visiting one?

Crystals are nature's power sources from the earth. All crystals have a very steady rate of vibration. We mine them for our pleasure, their beauty, and to enhance our energy. Do you have a favorite type of crystal? A favorite crystal color? Write about your relationship with any crystal(s) you may have.

Native cultures are very particular about taking crystals out of the earth. They do not use bulldozers and seem to have a sixth sense of when a crystal mine has given up its rocks and needs to rest. Then they leave the earth alone. This natural rhythm can apply to all daily life: when to "harvest" and when to let the "field" lie fallow. Write about any experiences with this natural rhythm of sowing and reaping in any area of your life.

Gems are the most valuable and beautiful crystals the earth offers. Do you have a favorite gem? Describe it and any experiences you have had with this gem.

Each element personality has a characteristic type of humor! Dry wit and earthy jokes describe earth element humor. Is this true for you? Do you consider yourself a funny person? Describe your sense of humor and any occasions when you have entertained a circle of friends and/or family.

Earth sometimes blows her top with volcanoes or earthquakes. These tectonic shifts under the earth or sea balance the planet even though they can cause great damage in the process. Have you experienced an earthquake or volcano? Describe your feelings and experiences. If you haven't personally experienced an earthquake or volcano, what are your thoughts and feelings about them?

Just as the earth can erupt, we may sometimes find ourselves ready to burst with anger. Do you personally have temper eruptions? What kinds of situations enrage you? Write a dialogue between your calm self and that angry self.

....
....
....
....
....
....
....
....
....
....
....
....
....
....
....
....
....
....
....
....
....
....
....
....
....
....
....

....
....
....
....
....
....
....
....
....
....
....
....
....
....
....
....
....
....
....
....
....
....
....
....
....
....
....
....
....

Do you know that dogs and other animals sense earthquakes and other weather changes before they occur? Have you ever had a dog or other animal warn you of an upcoming weather event? If you are familiar with this "early-warning system," describe the event and what happened. If you have never had such an experience, how do you gather your weather information? TV weather? Smartphone app? *Farmers' Almanac?*

Trees are natural wonders that provide shade, clean the air, and give beauty. They can also provide a climate record of growth, drought, and famine. Trees form the backbone of the Wood Wide Web—a phrase that describes how trees communicate with each other to warn of pests and to help conserve water during dry seasons. Write about your experiences with trees. Have you ever visited an old forest?

The Wood Wide Web—the idea that trees can communicate with each other, send warnings about dangers, and help conserve water during a dry spell—is beautifully described in a book called *The Hidden Life of Trees* by Peter Wohlleben. If you've read this book, what were your thoughts? If you haven't read it, grab a copy and start reading, then write about your reactions.

Forest bathing—consciously walking, sitting, or lying down in a forest to feel the peaceful and healing atmosphere—has become popular in recent years. We want to connect with the earth and the trees. Have you ever done this? What were your experiences? If you haven't practiced forest bathing before, try it out, then write about how it went.

....
....
....
....
....
....
....
....
....
....
....
....
....
....
....
....
....
....
....
....
....
....
....
....

The pyramids are monumental structural achievements from ancient times. They were built by many different cultures, most famously in Egypt. Are you curious about how ancient people erected them without machines? Some people hypothesize that ancient people knew how to harden sand: They created frames on top of frames, filled them with sand, and let it harden. Very efficient! What do you think of this possibility? How do you think it connects with the characteristics of earth signs?

What is the most comfortable place in your home? Why? Did you build this home? Did you buy it? Or do you rent it? The earth element usually feels best owning their own home, so they can improve it without restrictions and increase its value. Write a dialogue between you and your home—the furniture, comforts, and discomforts. What have you improved? What would you like to improve?

People on Planet Earth often measure success by how much material wealth they garner. Do you believe this is the best measure of success? Is material wealth important to you? What other ways might you use to measure success?

Earth colors are warm beige, browns, burgundy, black, dark blue, and yellow. Are these your favorite colors? Describe your wardrobe: Is it full of earth tones? Do you wear different colors for different seasons?

If the ruler of the world were an earth sign, what would be their most important contribution? Would you nominate an earth, fire, air, or water sign to lead the world? Why?

If you were a highly developed being from another planet and landed on Earth, what would be your most significant observations about the land, resources, technology, and people? Do you believe there are more advanced civilizations than on Planet Earth?

The twelve astrological signs we know today come from the twelve constellations arranged around the ecliptic of the sun's path. Astrologers observe these signs and interpret their effect on people and events. For example, an astrologer may note that as a Virgo, a person might be great at analysis but find it challenging to synthesize all the details. And a Scorpio may be drawn to jobs or a certain career where they can investigate people or subjects, but a corporate structure doesn't appeal to them. Through understanding your Sun sign, you have a unique window of insight into yourself and your life!

The prompts in this part will guide you through a deeper exploration of your Sun sign and the traits, relationship dynamics, and more that may be influenced by this sign. Reflect on how your career path may be impacted by your sign. Consider how a certain characteristic linked to your sign plays into how you handle conflict with friends. Through guided journaling, this part will help you get to know yourself better. Of course, there is much more to astrology than your personal Sun sign. If you are interested in knowing even more about your relationship with the cosmos, you can also look at the other signs in your birth chart, such as your ascendant sign. Or you may want to focus more deeply on general astrology, as well as your Sun sign and sign element, and revisit different prompts to see how your reflections may evolve. This is *your* astrological journey: Let it take you wherever you want to go!

PART THREE

GETTING TO KNOW YOUR SIGN

Capricorn is the last earth sign of the zodiac and the most enigmatic. Her symbol is a mythical creature called the sea goat (yes, despite the fact that Capricorn is an *earth* sign!). Through time, the goat has become the image for Capricorn's fearless ambition. And the sea element of the goat's fish tail symbolizes the profound spiritual aspect of Capricorn. A mythical, spiritual creature or a steadfast goat? Write your feelings toward these different parts of Capricorn's symbol and which one you feel most connected to.

The sun's entry into Capricorn is called the World Point, or, more commonly, the winter solstice. The winter solstice marks both the darkest part of the sun's journey (being the longest night of the year) as well as the beginning of the climb toward light. Many early religions celebrate the winter solstice. Christians call this time Christmas for the birth of Christ, who metaphorically brings us light. Do you celebrate the solstice? Write your feelings about this time of year. Do you feel depressed on the dark winter days? What do you do to encourage your own light?

If you imagine a goat climbing from crag to crag on a steep mountain, you can easily understand the drive and determination of Capricorn's personality! Does this describe you? Write about a time when you were determined to accomplish a goal even though the odds may not have been in your favor.

Capricorn is one of four cardinal signs, which begin a new season. Capricorn begins the winter season. Cardinal signs are marked by strong leadership, and Capricorn rules big business and hierarchies and is very comfortable working within these structures. Describe your ideal work position and your career goals. Is there a definite climb to the top involved?

....

....

....

....

....

....

....

....

....

....

....

....

....

....

....

....

....

....

....

....

....

....

....

....

....

....

....

....

....

....

....

Saturn is the farthest planet that people can see without the help of a telescope. And Saturn rules both structure and time. Ruled by this planet, Capricorn is usually comfortable with the passage of time. Many Capricorns feel that older is better. What are your feelings about getting older? Describe your images for each decade of life after thirty.

Age thirty is the end of what is known as the Saturn Return, which begins at age twenty-eight. It means that Saturn has made one whole circuit of your chart and returned to the position it was in when you were born. It is a coming-of-age transit. Have the years from twenty-eight to thirty passed for you? If so, what were they like? If they are still to come, how do you feel about them?

As an earth sign, a Capricorn's Saturn Return (the return of Saturn to the position when you were born) typically brings a settled feeling. Her feet are on the ground, and her choices are based on reality rather than wishes. Describe any real-world decision you are making or made during this time. If it is yet to come, do you have any concrete plans for life when it does?

Saturn is a serious planet and Capricorn's ruler, so those born under this sign are known for a serious approach to life. *But* they also have a dry wit and are very funny when considering life's foibles! What is the funniest situation you have ever found yourself in? How did it happen? What were your reactions both during the situation and as you retold it to people afterward?

Capricorn rules the skeletal structure of the body. All bones are her domain. It is best for Capricorn to do low-impact cardio or exercise that doesn't stress the joints. What are your exercise habits? Do you find that running is good for you or not the best sport?

Just as Capricorn is comfortable with aging, she is also a fan of classic styles and tailored attire. Even if working from home, do you prefer to dress for the office? A selection of business suits may hang ready to go in your closet. Describe your work wardrobe and anything you would like to purchase.

Capricorn is a work-centric person and may feel burned-out by bedtime. Do you have any rituals to relax your mind before sleep? What are they? If not, what rituals could you try? These may include eliminating electronic devices so your mind is not agitated by light and electromagnetic vibrations. Practice a relaxing ritual and record how it went.

Capricorn has a deep feeling for family. Tracing your family tree as far back as you can may give you insights into yourself and your family. It is also interesting to consider the Sun signs of different family members! Do you notice any consistent signs? Any connections between sign or element relationships?

In partnerships, Capricorn wants to know that the business partner or spouse is trustworthy with money and expenditures. Are you very mindful of keeping things equal with a partner? Of having open communication about money? How do you arrange finances?

Financial success is important to Capricorn; of course, even with careful planning, obstacles can come up. Describe a financial dilemma you have experienced. Did it involve a partner, or was it your personal experience? What was the primary lesson you learned from the experience?

Each Sun sign has a shadow side that appears throughout the person's life in order to allow mastery of the things that person struggles with. For Capricorn, the challenge can come from rigidly adhering to rules rather than considering feelings. Have you seen this trait in yourself? In what areas of life are you rigid? Have rules ever dampened your enjoyment and creativity? Conversely, describe a time when you let go and forgot about "shoulds" and "oughts" in favor of what you felt.

Which sign do you think is the most romantically compatible with Capricorns? What is their element? The traits of their sign? Why do you feel they are most compatible? Conversely, what sign do you think is most compatible with Capricorn in business? Why?

What sign (or multiple signs) do you feel does not align well with Capricorn's worldview? What is their element? The traits you feel would cause difficulties in a relationship with Capricorn? This relationship could be romantic or platonic.

In marriage, Capricorn is usually steadfast and loyal. She does not like to upset tradition or let go of the memories she shares with a mate. Is this true of you? Write about your experiences with long-term relationships.

Loyal Capricorn can be hesitant to leave a relationship, even when it may be what is best. Have you ever left a relationship? What was the most difficult part? What did you learn for the future? If you haven't left a relationship, knowing yourself, what do you feel would be the hardest part?

Many Capricorns love salty foods such as caviar, anchovies, and chips. Does this appeal to your palate? Write about your favorite dishes. Do you cook or prefer takeout?

What is your favored pace in life? Are you slow and measured or fast and erratic? Describe times when you rushed through something, then describe a time when you moved at a slower pace and planned carefully. Which experience best suited your nature?

As an earth sign, Capricorn may be devoted to gardening. She loves to plant annual bulbs and wait for them to sprout in the spring. Understanding this rhythm of the earth is second nature to most Capricorns. Is this true of you? Write about your feelings about gardening or tending the land.

As an earth sign, Capricorns tend to have very strong muscles. Consider weight training as part of your exercise plan: The act of lifting weights gives you a solidity that will keep you strong for life. Describe any experiences you have had with lifting weights. Do you enjoy this exercise? If you haven't lifted weights, give it a try, and write about how it went.

Capricorn is usually drawn to browns, black, winter white, and/or deep burgundy. These colors in a classic style suit the goat. What are your favorite colors? Do they differ from the ones listed?

All leather goods are ruled by Capricorn. Do you like wearing leather jackets or suits? Having leather accessories like wallets or bracelets? Describe your feelings about the materials that are your favorites during the winter months.

You can express your Capricorn creativity with modeling clay! Working with this earthy substance can be a hobby or stress reliever as you mold the clay into different shapes. Have you ever considered working with clay or making pottery? Write about your experiences with or thoughts about this form of creativity.

ADDITIONAL RESOURCES

Websites and Other Digital Resources

www.alabe.com

www.astro.com

www.astrodienst.com

www.lunarium.co.uk

www.changingofthegods.com

App: Co-Star

Books

Astrology, Psychology and the Four Elements by Stephen Arroyo

The Astrology of Fate by Liz Greene

Sun Signs by Linda Goodman

Relationship Signs by Linda Goodman

If You Want to Write by Brenda Ueland

The Artist's Way by Julia Cameron

The Hidden Life of Trees by Peter Wohlleben

The Hidden Power of Everyday Things by Constance Stellas, Julie Gillentine, and Jonathan Sharp

Sex Signs by Constance Stellas

The Astrological Guide to Self-Care by Constance Stellas

How to Be an Astrologer by Constance Stellas

The Little Book of Self-Care by Constance Stellas

BIBLIOGRAPHY

Arroyo, Stephen. *Astrology, Psychology and the Four Elements.* Davis, CA: CRCS, 1975.

Arroyo, Stephen. *Relationships & Life Cycles.* Vancouver, WA: CRCS, 1979.

Donath, Emma Belle. *Have We Met Before?* Tempe, AZ: American Federation of Astrologers, 1982.

Forrest, Steven. *The Book of Neptune.* Borrego Springs, CA: Seven Paws, 2016.

Forrest, Steven. *The Book of Fire.* Borrego Springs, CA: Seven Paws, 2019.

Green, Jeffrey Wolf. *Pluto: The Evolutionary Journey of the Soul, Volume I.* St. Paul, MN: Llewellyn, 1985.

Green, Jeffrey Wolf. *Pluto: The Soul's Evolution Through Relationships, Volume II.* St. Paul, MN: Llewellyn, 1997.

Greene, Liz. *The Astrology of Fate.* York Beach, ME: Weiser, 1984.

Hickey, Isabel M. *Astrology: A Cosmic Science.* Sebastopol, CA: CRCS, 2011.

Oken, Alan. *Soul Centered Astrology.* New York: Bantam, 1990.

Sargent, Lois Haines. *How to Handle Your Human Relations.* Tempe, AZ: American Federation of Astrologers, 1958.

Tester, Jim. *A History of Western Astrology.* New York: Ballantine, 1987.

Yott, Donald H. *Astrology and Reincarnation.* York Beach, ME: Weiser, 1989.

DEDICATION

To all those seeking the wisdom in their stars.

ACKNOWLEDGMENTS

I would like to thank Karen Cooper and everyone at Adams Media who helped with this book. To Brendan O'Neill, Katie Corcoran Lytle, Laura Daly, Julia Jacques, Sarah Doughty, Jo-Anne Duhamel, Julia DeGraf, and everyone else who worked on the manuscripts. To Frank Rivera, Priscilla Yuen, Colleen Cunningham, and Tess Armstrong for their work on the book's cover and interior design. I appreciated your team spirit and eagerness to dive into the riches of astrology.

Unique ways to refresh and restore— personalized for your

ZODIAC SIGN!

PICK UP OR DOWNLOAD YOUR COPIES TODAY!